Alexander
SELKIRK

WHO WAS...

Alexander
SELKIRK

Survivor on a
Desert Island

✳ SHORT BOOKS

Published in 2004 by
Short Books
15 Highbury Terrace
London N5 1UP

10 9 8 7 6 5 4 3 2

Copyright ©
Amanda Mitchison 2004

Map on page 42 courtesy of Bristol Reference Library.

A CIP catalogue record for this book
is available from the British Library.

ISBN 1-904095-79-8

Printed in Great Britain by
Bookmarque Ltd, Croydon, Surrey

To Connor, Rollo and Monty

CHAPTER ONE

It had been nine weeks since the sailors had set foot on land. Nine weeks of hard sailing, all down the coast of South America and then round the Horn with the storms pushing them south into the ice-bound waters of the Antarctic. They had met waves as high as houses and winds that would freeze a man's hands to the rigging and chill his heart to the core. The sailors had spat and cursed, they had greased their hands with whale blubber, tied sacking to their legs, tapped the weevils from their ships' biscuits and prayed for more rum.

Then finally they had come north into warmer waters. Two battered frigates, their rigging tattered, 50 men down with scurvy and three already dead. Now, after so many days, the rugged peaks of Juan

Fernandez loomed before them. Here, even though the mountains looked so forbidding, they knew they'd find clean water, fresh meat, and at last have a chance to rest.

Ten well-armed men rowed a small boat into the bay. The sailors were wary. There had been a fire up on the mountainside last night as they set anchor. Perhaps their French or Spanish enemies were hiding somewhere nearby. They cocked their muskets and scanned the island. But they had not rowed far before they heard the cries and shouting – a strange half-human, half-animal noise.

There on the beach, below the huge mountains and the forest, stood a tiny figure waving its arms frantically. The figure had the shape and proportions of a man, but it was entirely covered in fur, like a Barbary ape. The sailors crossed themselves. What was this thing? A new kind of animal? A monster?

They watched as the thing jumped up and down, waving its furry arms and pointing and hollering. Then it began to run. Yet it ran not like an ape, lolloping along with its arms trailing the ground, but like a man – only faster. When it stopped, it seemed to be pointing to a sandy landing spot. And as the sailors rowed into shore, they realised that the creature was in fact a human being, a wild-looking individual with a long woolly beard, and covered from head to foot in animal skins – and he was growing frantic with excitement.

The wild thing welcomed the sailors as long-lost friends, embracing each man in his big furry arms. He smelt very powerfully of goat. And as he hugged them all, he made strange sounds – not the grunts or snorts of an animal, but blurred bits of words, as if his tongue were stiff and his mouth unused to human speech.

The sailors strained their ears – the wild thing was not only speaking, but also doing so in a Scottish accent. For the wild thing was a sailor like them. He was in fact Alexander Selkirk, Scottish mariner and privateer, hale of heart and mind, and delighted to be rescued after spending four years and four months alone on a Pacific island. This book is about how Selkirk came to be stranded on the island and how he survived. It is the tale of what happened to the real Robinson Crusoe.

CHAPTER TWO

The church of Largo, in Fife, stood on a small windy hill overlooking the Firth of Forth, and boasted a small windy minister. Reverend Tulloch would keep his congregation at least three hours on a Sunday, and by the end of the sermon he had a voice like rusty rasp. He always kept sugared plums in his breeches and gargled honeyed tea on Sunday mornings, but nothing could keep out the croak. By the time he neared the end and was calling upon his lowly congregation of farmhands and fishermen to repent and save themselves from the burning pits of hell, his own throat always ached as if it, too, were on fire.

And this Sunday, like every Sunday, Reverend Tulloch's voice soared and scraped. He preached and implored. He cast his eyes up on high to the fine, stone-arched ceiling of the church and called down the wrath of the Lord God Almighty upon these loathsome sinners before him. Then he lowered his gaze and looked down on the ranks of bowed, grubby necks in the pews. His eyes scanned the rows, picking out his most frequent offenders: the swindling shrew-faced cheese-seller, fat Margaret the fornicator, and the red-faced, ginger-haired Mitchell brothers, whose often-used fists were almost as big as their seldom-used heads.

And then, quite suddenly, Reverend Tulloch noticed that one of the heads down beneath him was not bowed. Instead, the face – a young, fresh, blue-eyed face – was staring directly at him. What's more, the face showed no fear at all.

He should have expected as much. For the face belonged to Selcraig the cobbler's boy, that ruffian Alexander. He was a big-boned lad, bright as a button. His mother's darling and a seventh son – so bound to be lucky in life. But he was wayward, lawless, always ready to answer back. Never had any respect for his betters. Just look at him now! The minister blinked angrily. The lad even had the effrontery to grin at a man of the cloth!

Then Reverend Tulloch heard something. He paused and cocked his ear. There was a quite distinct splashing sound. Maybe a gutter was overflowing. Then came a second sound, just as distinct. It was the sound of muffled giggling, giggling accompanied by looks and whispering. The sound spread and rippled across his congregation, like wind over a field of oats. The minister looked again at Alexander Selcraig, for it was clearly from his pew that the giggling had started.

The lad was holding his prayer book with one hand, but the other hand was in his lap. A horrible thought occurred to the minister. Surely the boy would not have dared to make water in his church! He stared down at the youth with a look that should have frozen him to his bones. But Alexander just widened his grin and shrugged.

'Please you, sir,' he called out, 'but I was sore pressed and the sermon was over long.'

The following Sunday Alexander Selcraig, son of the cobbler and tanner John Selcraig, was called to appear before Reverend Tulloch and the elders of the church to account for his 'indecent conduct in church'. But Alexander didn't turn up. He had gone to sea.

***

On a fine Thursday morning, in the year of King William III's reign 1695, Alexander Selcraig set out from Largo, walking along the coast road down to Inverkeithing. In his leather purse he carried two changes of shirt, a horn spoon and cup, four blocks of cold oatmeal and two blood puddings. He also had two pieces of eight (old Spanish coins) stitched to the inside of his breeches by his loving mother. All his father had given him was advice: 'Cut your hair only in a storm, don't crack walnuts with your teeth, and never trust an Englishman!'

Thus equipped, Alexander felt ready to face the world. He walked along the road with a sense of victory. Ever since he could remember he had always wanted to go to sea. Finally after all these years, thanks to his behaviour in church on Sunday, his father had given way and let him go, saying there was certainly no hope for his son if he stayed on in the village. John Selcraig had always scoffed at his son's ambition. Everyone knew that seamen were prison flotsam, desperate, pox-ridden thieves and ruffians.

And the sea was a cruel mistress – if she didn't claim you for herself, a putrid fever or the scurvy surely would. When did you ever see an old seaman? Hardly ever. When did you ever see an old seaman with teeth? Never at all. John Selcraig told his son to find himself an honest trade. There was no good to be had from running after fool's gold.

But, for Alexander, it wasn't just the lure of gold. Of course to return home laden with plate and pearls and barrels of claret would be a fine thing, but what he wanted most was adventure and excitement. Over the oceans there were lands stranger than any of his dreams. Lands made of ice where it was always winter. Lands so hot the rivers boiled and the leaves on the trees grew taller than a man. Lands where the mountains belched fire and there roamed animals with noses that reached the ground, and necks that stretched to the tops of trees. There were great forests with savage cats as large as ponies and striped like a barber's pole. There were wild men with heads growing out from their breast bones and gold rings in their noses. There were women with three breasts and long beards. He knew it was all true, for he had seen the drawings in a pamphlet.

***

Two days later, it was a tired and bedraggled Alexander Selcraig that finally arrived at the port of Leith, in Edinburgh. Outside Largo he had managed to get a lift in a cart to Inverkeithing. But the weather had soured on him. Rain, and then drizzle, followed by more rain, and then the road had turned to mud. At Queensferry he had crossed the Firth of Forth in a rocky little rowing boat and, as the waves splashed against his back, he had realised that he couldn't have got any wetter if he had swum across the estuary.

Afterwards there had been another long muddy trudge to Edinburgh, which he had always believed to be a grand city, full of rich and magnificent houses. Instead, when he arrived, he had found himself wandering through a maze of dirty crowded streets with stinking gutters and buildings black as tar. So he was most relieved when he reached the sea air down at Leith docks.

The quayside was very busy. A large frigate was being loaded up. Barrels were being rolled precariously down gangplanks and men, ghostly white as millers, were heaving in huge sacks of flour and rice.

Alexander stepped gingerly between the piles of nets and coils of rope and made his way to the loading bay. Sitting on a metal pommel beside one of the gangplanks, he saw a huge man with strange blue and red drawings all over him: hearts, anchors, a frigate on his left forearm, a unicorn's head on the side of his neck. Only the man' s right arm had no drawings and that was because he had no right arm. Instead, the right shirtsleeve was neatly tucked into his waistcoat pocket. Alexander wondered. Perhaps he had had a fall from the rigging, or been crushed under a barrel? Or maybe the arm had been smashed by shot, and then sawn off by the ship's surgeon and the stump dipped in burning pitch?

The quartermaster, who always kept an eye on idle youths wandering on the quay, knew that he was being stared at. He turned to Alexander, spat a brown gobbet of tobacco out into the harbour water and said, 'Lad, look sharp! You want work?'

Alexander replied that he was indeed hoping to join a ship. The boatswain looked Alexander up and down. He checked the boy's palms to see if he had been branded a thief, and then he opened his mouth and peered inside. He noted Alexander's full set of teeth, and gave an approving grunt.

'A Landsman, then. Not been to sea, boy, eh?' asked the boatswain.

'Nae, sir,' replied Alexander.

'Then away aloft!'

Alexander stared back dumbfounded. What did the fellow mean?

'Up the mainstay!' barked the man and he pointed to a small platform at the top of the mast.

The only way to reach the top was by the 'ratlines' – the rope webbing between the cables that held the mast in place. Alexander took off his shoes and stockings and started to climb. Up and up he went, holding tight to the black greasy rungs and not daring to look down.

The further he climbed the more he felt the swaying motions of the boat and the wind growing stronger, pulling the breath from his mouth and making his shirt bellow out like a sail. He climbed on upward, the wind now pulling very hard, as if it wanted to prise him away from the rigging. Alexander felt his spine bending and his shoulders and elbows straining against the force of the wind. If he fell now his body would be smashed to pulp like a blackberry.

He shut his eyes, repeated the first few lines of the Lord's Prayer, drew in his breath and climbed on up the rigging. When he reached the top of the ratlines, he clambered up clumsily on to the platform. Here, with his joints aching and his bowels slippery with fear, he hugged tight to the mast. He knew this didn't look very dignified to the seamen down below but he didn't care. At least he was alive – even if he would still have to climb back down again.

When the wind eased off a little and his stomach settled, Alexander opened his eyes and looked out over the Firth of Forth to the rolling green hills of Fife. Then he turned to look down. Immediately below he could see tiny, pinsized figures scurrying about their business on deck. The pinsized one-armed boatswain wasn't even watching.

Eventually Alexander climbed over the side of the platform and started out down the ratlines. But he came down differently. This time he chose the other side of the ship, so that the wind was behind him, pushing him into the rigging rather than pulling him away.

From that day on he would always go aloft on

the windward side. He had learnt his first lesson of seamanship.

CHAPTER THREE

In the years that followed Alexander became a true sailor. Alexander Selkirk, as he now called himself – for the old boatswain had written down his name wrong and he had grown used to the new version – came to know every sea, from the great swirling eddies of the North Atlantic, to the treacherous reefs of the East Indies.

He soon lost his fear of heights, and by the end of his first long voyage he could run along the yardarms like a squirrel. He became handy, learning to splice rope and sew his own clothes and carve his jacket buttons from anything around – even cheese rind. He loved the foreign ports and the women of the quayside taverns who taught him to whisper 'I love you' in a hundred different languages. He also bought exotic pets and there were always parrots, iguanas or aggressive little Vervet monkeys in his berth. The creatures never lasted long, but Alexander grew fond of them and always shed a tear or two before he handed the carcasses over to the cook.

Alexander changed. He developed a rolling gait and an iron digestion. He could sleep through the noise of the caulking hammers and the screeching of the rigging in a high wind. His body hardened, his skin cracked, his forearms became broad and sinewy with pulling ropes. He lost teeth to scurvy and three toes and two finger joints to frostbite. He became accustomed to the stink of bilge and the foul air below deck. At night, he lay down to sleep cheek by jowl with cut-throats and thieves. And the violent ways of his companions rubbed off on him.

But if the sea coarsened his temper, it also refined his instincts. Like any good seaman Alexander could smell a storm brewing, and predict a change of wind from the slightest slackness in a sail. He also had an acute sense of foreboding. He knew when danger was near, when his ship was steering into hidden reefs, or pack-ice lay ahead. Several times in harbour he had felt a dull unease about the ship he was supposed to be joining and refused to go on board. Months later, he would learn that she had sunk, drowning the entire crew. It seemed as if his mother was right – seventh sons did indeed have second sight.

Alexander never took this special gift for granted and valued it above all things. A sailor needs all the good luck he can find. Others might carry charms and lockets, but Alexander relied on his nose. And, until now, his nose had always been right.

But today, standing on deck of the *Cinque Ports* on a sunny February morning in the year 1704, with the blue waters of the Pacific before him and the craggy mountains of Juan Fernandez soaring over his shoulder, Alexander didn't feel so sure.

He pressed his finger against the main mast. His nail sank in easily. He picked at the wood, and it came away, crumbling softly in his hand. He knew the wood in the hull was just as bad, and the nails were iron-sick. If the ship sailed this morning, as Captain Stradling had ordered, she would surely never make it back round the Horn. He had chosen a bad ship.

Back in Bristol, the year before, when he had joined up as sailing master – for he had done well at sea and was now an officer – he had known that the *Cinque*

Ports was a poorly made ship. But he had reckoned that as long as she could get them to the Spanish mainland, he would make his fortune.

For this time, Alexander was no mere wage-earning sailor. He had become a privateer, signed up for his own share of the booty. It was a fine distinction – privateer or pirate. Alexander's ship had a letter of commission from the Admiralty, giving government approval to the mission. If the crew were captured by the Spanish, they would be punished as British citizens, i.e. they would be taken as prisoners, rather than hanged as common criminals.

But, whatever official documents they may have carried with them, Alexander and his men were pirates at heart and bent on plunder. They traded stories of Spanish galleons groaning with gold from the mines of Chile and Peru. They daydreamed about coastal trading posts too sleepy to defend themselves and little settlements of huts where savages were so awash with gold they bent the precious metal into children's toys and fish hooks.

Standing on the deck now, with no money in his sea-chest, he cursed himself for a fool. The *Cinque Ports*, commanded by the stubborn old sea dog

Thomas Stradling, had only just scraped round the Horn and had then sailed north to the islands of Juan Fernandez to recover from the ordeal. From there the ship had headed for the Spanish coast, but the privateers, being too slow for the enemy ships, had captured barely any gold.

With their luck down, they had returned once again to Juan Fernandez, only to find that the stores they had hidden – including several kegs of brandy – had disappeared. This discovery had enraged Captain Stradling. And Stradling's bad temper had stayed. This wasn't like Alexander's whiplash rages, flaring up suddenly but over just as fast. Captain Stradling's black moods were of the lingering, malevolent sort. No amount of fresh food or pleasant island air could restore his humour to its ordinary, workaday cussedness.

***

And today was no exception. The Captain had been finding fault and snarling like a caged dog all morning. Alexander watched Stradling stride down the deck towards him.

'Look lively Mr Selkirk! The wind is turning!'

Alexander gazed beyond Stradling's shoulder to where the still water of the bay met the curve of the shoreline. The mountains gave good shelter – the bay would be a fine place to keel the ship over and scrape the weeds off the hull.

'My compliments sir,' replied Alexander continuing to stare out into the bay, 'but we don't sail today.'

'We don't sail today!' cried Stradling, 'What the deuce do you mean? I have said that we leave today. These are my orders! And Mr Selkirk I would remind you of your duties. You are not to be gawping like a mooncalf and picking cracks in the mast.'

'Aye sir,' replied Alexander, continuing to stare over the Captain's shoulder. 'But the wood is rotten. The ship is naught but worm.' And he crumbled a segment of the soft wood between his fingers and let it fall to the deck in front of Captain Stradling's feet.

Stradling snarled, 'Merely a weak spot Mr Selkirk, every ship has her weak spots. Just as every crew has her insolent rascals.'

Alexander ignored the slight. 'Sir we have been pumping her day and night all this fortnight past. We must refit the hull. There is good timber on the island;

she could be ready in a month. Should she sail today, she'll go down in the first high sea.'

'Mr Selkirk, I do not need to be told about the condition of the hull! I have sailed on ships in worse states of disrepair.'

'Very well sir,' replied Alexander 'but I have not. I am proud to be alive and I wish to remain so.'

'Will you hold your tongue Mr Selkirk!' shouted the captain.

'That I will not.' Alexander's neck flushed with rage.

'Then confound you for a fool Mr Selkirk!' exclaimed Stradling. 'I am the captain and I tell you that we sail today.'

'Aye, very well sir,' replied Alexander. 'And I am the quartermaster and if she sails today, she sails without me. I'd sooner perish here than go to the bottom in such company!'

'Very well!' said Stradling, his eyes ablaze. 'If that is your wish Mr Selkirk, I am sure you can be accommodated!'

And the captain turned on his heel and shouted over to a couple of young hands climbing down the rigging.

'Boxer! Mr Selkirk's chest to the pinnace! O'Flannery! Have cook prepare two day's rations. And look sharp!'

Boxer and O'Flannery scuttled below to do the captain's bidding, but Alexander remained standing on deck with his arms crossed. He felt strangely excited. The men would surely follow him. They knew the ship was rotten, they must realise she couldn't sail. Yet, as the men hauled out his sea-chest and the creaking pulleys lowered the rowing boat down into the water, Alexander was left alone. Nobody spoke up or approached him. Even the ship's carpenter, who knew the bottom of the ship better than anyone, had become wide-eyed and mute.

But Alexander was a proud man, and he remained standing on the deck staring out into the bay, his face as still as a sphinx. He felt like cursing his frightened seamates – they could share a watery grave with that old dog for all he cared! Then he bade a silent farewell to the *Cinque Ports* and climbed down the rope into the small rowing boat. Behind him clambered Stradling. The captain, it seemed, wasn't going to miss the opportunity to see his quartermaster marooned.

The men rowed hard and the pinnace moved slowly across the bay. No one felt inclined to talk. When the pinnace reached the shore, Stradling remained in his seat and gave a curt nod to Alexander who climbed out of the boat without looking back. The seamen heaved the sea-chest on to the beach. Here, with embarrassed smiles and handshakes, they bade their old companion farewell and waded back out to the boat.

Alexander sat down on the sea-chest, kicked his feet casually to and fro, and stared impassively out to sea where the pinnace was setting off back to the *Cinque Ports*. His first thought was 'no more bloaters'. A golden, freshly fried bloater washed down with rum was the very best start to the day. But you needed a boat and line to catch bloaters and a griddle to fry them. And now he had no griddle and no boat and no rum.

Alexander looked out at the little boat in the bay and felt a tightness in his chest. This might be the last boat he saw for some time. And these might be the last men he saw for some time, maybe for a long time, maybe forever. He could be stranded on Juan Fernandez for months, or years, or decades. He could perish here – there was no saying what horrors lurked up in the forest. And it would be a grisly rumless death, with no one to bury him, no one to tell his family what had become of him. No one to miss him.

He jumped off the sea-chest, ran down the beach. Dignity be damned! There was still time – the boat wasn't yet 50 yards away. Alexander ran out into the water, his arms flailing.

'Sir! Sir!' he shouted, with the water up to his waist 'I've changed my mind. I'll be sailing with you.'

The sailors rested their oars and looked up, waiting for the order to turn the boat around. But Stradling was resolute. He cupped his hands round his mouth and yelled back.

'Well I have not changed mine! Stay where you are and may you starve!'

On board the *Cinque Ports* the carpenter winced and crossed himself.

CHAPTER FOUR

Alexander waded slowly back out of the water, shook himself like a dog, and, shivering slightly, returned to his sea-chest. He had a terrible desire to throw stones at the rowing boat as it retreated into the bay, but he knew that would hardly encourage the Captain to come back for him. So instead he simply sat down on the sea-chest.

As the morning wore on, Alexander watched miserably as the *Cinque Ports* pulled up anchor, unfurled her sails and slowly tacked out of the bay. Eventually the ship's main mast dipped under the horizon, but Alexander still didn't lose hope. He was convinced that Stradling would be back, though it might be several hours before his temper cooled.

Alexander opened his sea-chest. He was well

provided for. He had spare clothes, his bedding, his musket, a kettle, a knife, a hatchet, a pound of gunpowder, a Bible, books on navigation, mathematical instruments, his tankard and a pouch of tobacco. And, nesting on top of his bedding, he found, wrapped in a grubby bundle of cloth, a haunch of salt pork, a large bag of broken ship's biscuit, another of dried oats, and a twist of parchment containing a small, foul blob of rancid butter.

Alexander sniffed at the meat and smiled. Cook's two days of rations were most generous and the meat wasn't too rotten. With hope rising in his heart, Alexander flipped open the lid on his tankard. But it was empty. No ale, no rum, nothing.

In the afternoon Alexander set up camp. He gathered firewood, collected fresh water from the stream, hacked a wedge of pork off the bone – the stuff was hard as wood – and boiled it up in his kettle. As he sat nibbling at biscuits and skimming the yellow scum off the top of the boiling pork, he watched the bay. But the *Cinque Ports* did not return.

When night fell, Alexander took his bedding out of his chest and curled up on the ground. He shut his eyes, but having spent weeks on the ship, the ground felt strangely still and the lack of motion made it hard for him to sleep. The island was ringing with mysterious noises. The waves breaking on the shore, the wind swooping down the mountain and whistling through the forests, the roar of waterfalls, the occasional crash of trees and boulders. Then, suddenly, just as he was beginning to feel snug and warm by his fire, there came a terrible cry – a violent wailing noise. Something very wild and very large was calling out in anger or pain.

Alexander sat up, the sweat poured down his face and his body went rigid with terror. The sound was definitely not human. Were monsters of the deep, or demons of the forest coming to get him? In the dark he groped for his sea-chest, brought out his musket and released the catch.

He crouched there in the dark for what seemed an age, but the monster came no nearer and eventually the screams subsided. And finally, as dawn rose, Alexander fell asleep slumped over his cocked musket.

When he awoke, he was puzzled to find himself lying on a beach. Then, with a horrible jolt, he remembered the events of the day before, and his argument with Stradling. He looked out into the bay.

There was still no sign of the *Cinque Ports*.

He cooked the oats up into porridge, which he ate straight from the kettle. Then he went for a walk up and down the shore. Here, among an outcrop of rocks near to the woods, he found a cave – dank and narrow with a thick layer of bat droppings under foot. If the weather turned bad he might have to sleep here. Perhaps it was a home to those monsters he had heard at night?

He wanted to go into the forest, but he dared not venture inland in case the ship should return while he was out of sight. So for the rest of the day he just sat on the beach. Sometimes he smoked his pipe, other times he nibbled at the ship's biscuits. The time passed very slowly and the sun seemed to creep across the sky at a snail's pace. He tried to stop himself looking out to sea too often, for the ship was never there.

And so the next few days passed. Alexander sat and waited and smoked and nibbled. When cook's supplies ran out, he just sat and smoked. A strange weariness had overtaken him and even the idea of walking down to the water's edge and back seemed too much. He had to force himself to his feet to gather water. Every night he was scared out of his wits by the monsters of the deep, but they never came and claimed him.

Gradually Alexander gave up hope of being rescued. He went over the argument with Stradling a thousand times in his head and cursed himself for losing his temper. He was filled with regret. (In fact this was ill-founded; Alexander had been right about the state of the ship – the *Cinque Ports* was ship-wrecked, and Straddling and the other survivors were later imprisoned in Lima by the Spanish.)

He longed for company. Sometimes he found himself muttering to stones or rock pools. Sometimes he despaired completely, and even contemplated ending his life with one quick shot of the musket. But then the same thought always deterred him: there was no one to give him a decent burial. He had never felt so alone.

Eventually it was hunger that saved Alexander from his black moods. For several days after cook's rations were finished, he felt no inclination to eat. But one morning he woke up ravenous and went down to the shore and tickled a couple of small silvery fish from the water. He roasted them on a fire and devoured them, still only half-cooked. But it was strange to eat his food unsalted and with no bread or ship's biscuit.

The fish felt soft in his mouth, and the insipid flavour made him want to gag.

Soon he gave up on fish – he just hated the taste and found that they made his bowels loose. Instead, he feasted on the local crayfish which were the size of lobsters and hid under the rocks along the seashore. Then one day he decided to try and kill an elephant seal. He had never seen such large and ungainly creatures before. Some of the males were 16 feet long and had bodies as wide as trees. Their fat necks and great ponderous noses reminded him of the rich Fife farmers he had glimpsed passing in carriages when he was a child.

But killing elephant seals was hardly 'hunting'. Alexander loaded his musket, walked down to the water's edge, pointed his gun at the head of a small female lolloping along the sand and shot her in the brain. The seal slumped down silently and closed her eyes, whereupon a nearby male raised itself on to its fore-fins and let out a fearsome roar.

For a moment Alexander was startled. Then he started to laugh. Soon he found he couldn't stop – he laughed on and on until tears rolled down his cheeks and his ribs ached.

For at last he had found the source of his fears. The elephant seal's roar was the sound that had terrorised him throughout the long nights. Here were his monsters of the deep! He marvelled that his mind could play such tricks on him.

From that day on Alexander slept soundly at night. He also ate better. Elephant seal meat, which he cut into thin strips and roasted on the fire, was a little fishy, but almost as good as mutton. And, it was the beginning of the breeding season: the elephant seals were coming onto the shore in increasing numbers. They were so easy to kill; they looked fearsome, but they were really very slow and stupid. Alexander soon found that if he walked straight towards a bull elephant seal it would raise itself up on its forefins and roar at him with its mouth wide open, whereupon he could fire his musket straight down its pink throat. When he ran out of ammunition, he took to approaching the creatures from behind, killing them with a hatchet before they turned round. He also discovered that the elephant seals' stiff black whiskers made excellent toothpicks.

Gradually, Alexander began to venture inland. He had already seen all the island from the sea. So he knew it was large – a rough triangle about 15 miles long and five miles wide. From a distance Juan Fernandez had looked like a steep mass of rock and impossibly dense undergrowth with a ridge of high craggy mountains down the middle. But closer at hand it proved a far more accommodating environment. The forest that reached down to the edge of the beach was made up of cotton-wood trees with massive trunks and huge pimento pepper trees as tall as church spires. Underneath, the forest floor was very fertile. Alexander stamped through the undergrowth and picked turnips and parsnips which were just like the ones at home, but smaller and juicier. Tufts of watercress grew in the streams.

Further inland he found cabbage palms, tall trees which produced a sweet white fruit. But what he enjoyed most was a type of small black plum. The fruit was sharp and delicious and very hard to find – the trees grew right up on the steep, rocky sides of the mountains.

To the west, beyond the forest lay a sandy, grassland area where the ground was pitted with burrows dug by pardels, strange puffin-like creatures. He also saw albatrosses, hawks, owls, pintados, tiny humming birds the size of bees and a bird resembling a sparrow but with a red breast. And more importantly for Alexander, the island was also inhabited by animals: rats, cats and goats.

He had never imagined that goats could be so useful. He ate the meat, cured the skins and stretched out the cartilage to make it into thread. Once he even tried to use the innards. He pulled out the intestines, washed them out in seawater and then tried to stuff some chopped up meat into the long slippery tube. It seemed to take forever and the membrane kept breaking or sliding out of his hands. After a while, he gave up – even on a desert island, life was too short to make sausages.

Soon Alexander noticed the approach of winter. Every day the sky grew a little darker and the showers of rain were heavier. At night he now found himself shivering under his bedding. What would he do if very cold weather took hold? Certainly he didn't like the idea of spending a winter in the dank, bat-filled cave. He would have to build himself a house in the forest.

About a mile from the beach there was a small, sunlit clearing in the trees, with a stream nearby. The perfect spot. So he heaved his sea chest through the undergrowth, cursing and muttering as he broke through the tangle of undergrowth and bumped against huge roots.

How was he to build a house? Alexander started with the job he knew best. He shot and skinned several goats and then, after he had scraped off all the fat, he softened the hides by soaking them in salt water and then stretched them to dry on racks in the sun. After a few days, the goatskins were cured – the leather supple and the fur still soft and shiny. In his father's tannery, Alexander had never worked with such fine, fresh skins. They would keep him warm this winter.

The other tasks proved harder. Alexander was not a skilled carpenter. With his hatchet, he broke off some large pimento branches but he had neither saw nor hammer, and his only nails were a few rusty stubs that he pulled free from his sea-chest. So he made do with his knife and hatchet, wedging the joints into place and then binding them with bits of reed and threads pulled from one of his woollen stockings.

After several days, two rickety structures emerged. Alexander thatched them with long grass from the hills and lined the walls with his goatskins. In the bigger hut he used the last of the nails to build a sleeping platform and placed his bedding and more goatskins on top. The smaller hut was to be his kitchen and smokehouse and here he constructed a spit out of pimento wood, so that he could roast goat and seal.

In the kitchen Alexander experimented. He soon grew used to eating his food without salt and found other ways to add flavour – in the woods there was black pepper (which also served as a cure for flatulence). He made cray-fish broth and jellied eel. He cut goats' flesh into thin slices, laid it in strips over a very slow fire and sealed the entrance to the hut with a goat skin. After a few hours the strips would turn black with the smoke. He could keep this cured meat for weeks, and he took to chewing it between meals, as a substitute for tobacco.

Alexander was lucky, for, on the day he finished lining the walls of his bedroom hut, snow started to fall. The air had suddenly grown very cold, and gusts of freezing wind whistled down from the mountain. He quickly gathered wood, lit a fire in his sleeping hut and crawled in under the goatskins on his bed. The hut proved very snug, but also very smelly because of the goatskins. Alexander burned pimento and allspice wood, both of which produced a fragrant smoke, though the whiff of old goat never quite went away.

But Alexander became accustomed to the smell, and grew to like his huts. He decorated the walls with branches of pimento, and carved wooden ornaments to put round his bed. In the winter he hunkered down inside for hours, listening to the patter of hail on the ground while he chipped away at blocks of wood or read his navigation books and his Bible. He practised charting the movements of the stars with his quadrant and set square. He also learnt psalms off by heart and, every morning and evening, he prayed and recited out loud so that he would not entirely lose the power of speech. He often found himself moved to tears by passages of the Bible. In the past Reverend Tulloch had put him off religion, but now he began to wonder more about God and to ask questions that had barely crossed his mind before. Why had he been placed on this earth? What was God's purpose in leaving him on the island? Had he always been destined to such a peculiar fate? Was this why he had never married?

To stop his mind from dwelling on such thoughts, Alexander sometimes needed to get away from his huts. He needed to run till he could feel his blood hammer in his ears and his heart pound. He needed the thrill of danger and the rush of wind in his face. And on the crags of Juan Fernandez, with the waves smashing against the rocks and the rain thudding on his shoulders, he finally found what he was looking for. Alexander discovered the joys of chasing the wild mountain goats – though the sport was very nearly to kill him.

The Island
Juan Fernandes

CHAPTER FIVE

Alexander stood gasping for breath with his back pressed against the trunk of a pine tree and his feet slowly sliding down into the loose, mossy black soil. He had run so hard, leaping the narrow paths of the cliff face, that he felt as if someone had punched him in the side. The young goat had run hard too – though you wouldn't think it to see her now, grazing quietly on a clump of bushes at the edge of the cliff. The goat, a young female with a pretty, dappled coat and a dark triangular mark between the eyes, nibbled on, seemingly quite unconcerned. But she knew that the game wasn't finished – for they were old combatants. She was one of his best runners, sly and fast, wriggly as an eel. She had three notches in her right ear to mark the three times that he had caught her, and each time she had repaid Alexander with bites and kicks in the chest.

The goat raised its head and looked over to Alexander's tree. Goats, Alexander had learnt, had a weary, schoolmasterly way of looking at you – as if their minds were on far higher things. Black Triangle was no exception. She stared her schoolmasterish stare, but then something extraordinary happened: she closed one eye and opened it again. Was he losing his mind? Had he been alone on the island too long? He could have sworn that she had winked at him!

Suddenly Alexander dived forward, grabbing Black Triangle with both arms. But as he rolled on to the animal something gave from under him. It wasn't the slow slide of earth crumbling away, for, as he quickly realised, there was no land underneath him. The goat had been partly perching on an overhanging bush which now, branch by branch, was breaking under his weight. Still grappling with the goat and trying to control the flailing hooves, Alexander had no free hands to grab at the vegetation. He heard the crashing of branches and somewhere from the tumble of human and goat's limbs, came a terrified scream. The scream, he realised, must be coming from him. For the goat couldn't be screaming – its teeth were sunk deep in his arm. As he and the goat tumbled over the edge, he felt no pain, just a rush of fear. But the scream continued, echoing down the gully as the man and his quarry fell down the mountain into darkness.

***

When Alexander awoke the afternoon sun was shining straight on to his face. Fierce stabbing pains shot up his legs and arms. He was breathing with difficulty – his chest felt dented as if he had been rolled over by a barrel. He tried to raise himself onto his elbows, to see if every part of him was still there, but his head reeled. He lay down again and watched the light coming through the trees. High above the foliage he could see the cliff top from which he had slipped. He wriggled his fingers and toes – they all seemed to work. And yet there was blood everywhere – a great brown sticky puddle all around him.

He wondered how long he had been there in the foot of the gully. A few hours? A day? Or, God forbid, two days? Certainly long enough for all this blood to coagulate. Alexander turned his head to try and relieve the pain in his shoulders. His cheek touched fur and he realised he was lying on top of the goat. The creature was dead, its guts spilt on the ground. The poor goat had broken his fall.He had to be grateful. Alexander grinned – he had certainly won this last chase with Black Triangle. The luck of the seventh son had not run out.

All that day and the night that followed, Alexander lay on his back in the gully. When he realised he had urinated in his breeches he hardly cared, he just lay there unable to move and drifting in and out of sleep. But the night was cold, and he knew he wouldn't survive if he stayed out much longer. So the following morning he forced himself on to his knees and made his way slowly and painfully back up out of the gully, and through the forest to his huts. It took him most of the morning – a good mile he must have dragged himself, resting every few yards, and almost crying with the effort. When he finally arrived at his clearing, he crawled in under the goatskins on his bed and vowed that he would be more careful in future.

***

46

For ten days Alexander remained in his bed, getting up only to relieve himself or to collect water or cured seal meat from the straw roof of the cookhouse. But gradually, day by day, the pain lessened and his body recovered. Soon he was able to move his head without the forest seeming to lurch around him. And by the 11th day he was back on his feet and feeling well again.

From then on Alexander was more cautious on the cliffs. He also finally found a way to clear the rats from his hut. There had always been a few of them scuttling round the huts. But, after his accident, an invasion had begun. Every day there were more. The rats sensed his weakness and grew insolent, nibbling at the skin on his feet, picking at the tender scabs on his knees and elbows, scuttling over his stomach with their long earthworm tails.

On one occasion he woke up to find one dangling from his hand, like a bell-ringer on belfry rope. The rats felt no fear. He would try to shoo them away, or throw pieces of wood at them. They would stare back at him, blink slowly and lollop off. Then they would wait. The minute he began to drift back to sleep, he would hear a rustling noise and soon feel their small, sharp teeth biting into him again.

He knew that there was only one answer to the problem: cats. So, as soon he was able to, he killed another goat. He cut its liver into cubes and put some out near the nest of a young tabby with a litter of tiny kittens. The next day he put out more liver, a little further from the cat's nest. So he continued, every day putting the meat a little nearer to his huts. Within a week the cat and her kittens had moved in – and the rats had moved out.

Alexander also decided it was time to tame a few goats – for if he had another accident and became unable to chase goats he needed to have a supply of meat and milk. So he caught four kids, cut the tendons in their fetlocks and hobbled them to a post outside his hut.

Now Alexander's clearing was more like a farm-yard, and the animals made his life a little less lonely. He named the kittens after the Old Testament prophets, and he busied himself teaching them tricks. Kitten Obadiah learnt to clap his paws, and Deuteronomy could do a backwards roll. Alexander was particularly proud of Samuel's party piece – he could balance a piece of chopped liver on his nose and then flick it into his mouth using his tongue, without the help of his paws.

Alexander taught the kittens to dance. By the time they were cats they could totter on their hind legs while their master whistled a hornpipe. Sometimes even the hobbled goats would join in by jiggling their tethers, and Alexander would smile to himself and wonder at his unexpected talent. Maybe when he returned to Scotland he could set himself up as a dancing master...

Yet maybe he would not return. Would a ship ever rescue him? There was nothing he could do but wait. Certainly he wouldn't perish here from cold or hunger. And as long as he was healthy, he could keep going on Juan Fernandez. As his supplies ran out, Alexander discovered that he could always make do with what was on the island. When his tinderbox stopped working, he learnt to start fires by rubbing two bits of pimento wood together. When his knife wore out, he found some metal hoops from an old barrel cast up on the shore and he beat them into blades with a stone.

Bit by bit Alexander's clothing disintegrated. He had a roll of linen in his sea chest, so he made himself new shirts and sowed the seams with wool that he had unravelled from an old sock. He also made himself a cap, breeches and a jacket out of goatskins, sowing them together with goat sinew, and using an old nail as a needle. When his shoes fell to pieces, he simply went bare foot.

As the months passed, and then the years, Alexander looked wilder and woollier. His cheeks glowed and his hair shone, for it was a healthy life chewing turnips and chasing goats.

The melancholy that had affected him in the early days gradually lifted, and by the time he had been on the island eight months – and he knew it was eight months for he had notched up every day that passed on two cotton tree trunks near the clearing – he began to feel at peace with himself. After the first year and a half on the island had passed, he found he could stay inland, away from the beach, for an entire day.

And yet there were the gloomy days, days when he would sit and sulk inside his hut, stroking his cats. The cats of course had multiplied – there were so many he ran out of Old Testament prophets – and at night they would drape themselves in a great, warm, furry heap on his goatskin bed.

So now Alexander never worried about being nibbled by rats. Instead he developed a new pre-occupation. He became convinced that, if he died, his pet cats would consume his body. He tried to comfort himself with the thought that at least the cats would have the good manners to wait for him to die before they embarked on their feast. But the idea of being eaten haunted him.

And sometimes, looking out on to the empty ocean, he despaired of ever being rescued. He not only needed a ship to drop anchor in the bay, but it had to be the *right* ship. He had decided that, if French corsairs passed by, even though they were the enemy, he would give himself up. But he knew he must avoid the Spanish galleons at all cost, otherwise he would end his days working in chains down a gold mine in Peru. The Spanish never liked to release prisoners who might return home and pass on their knowledge of the Americas to others.

Twice the Spanish came ashore on Juan Fernandez, and twice Alexander was nearly caught. The first time it was his own fault. The Spanish sailors had made a small fire on the beach and Alexander was creeping through the edge of the forest to spy on the men, when suddenly he cracked some twigs underfoot. The Spanish sailors looked up, spied the wild-looking man and shot at him. Alexander ran back into the forest and with the sailors running and hollering behind him. But he was as fast as a mountian hare, and his pursuers soon turned back.

The second visit was worse. This time Alexander was unaware that a Spanish crew had come ashore and he was wandering down to the beach, when he suddenly caught sight of the campfire. The sailors shouted to him, but Alexander turned and ran back immediately into the forest. The Spanish sailors chased after him, firing their muskets.

He tried to divert the sailors by taking a path up the mountainside, but they were close on his trail and eventually, in desperation, he ran back to his huts and clambered up one of the cottonwood trees at the edge of the clearing. He had only just got to his hiding place when the sailors arrived. They shouted and fired shots into the huts and the nearby bushes, but it never occurred to them to look upwards. Eventually they gave up searching, killed two of the hobbled goats and tied them to a stick to carry back to the beach. Before the sailors left, one man urinated at the bottom of the tree where Alexander was hiding.

After this narrow escape, Alexander vowed to keep a more careful eye on the sea and he found himself a lookout post on a small ridge up on the mountain. He climbed every day and sat scanning the horizon.

But he saw no ships. Over months and then years, Alexander continued to visit his lookout. He would sit and watch the clouds scudding over the hills. He learnt the habits of the different birds and how the winds could change the colour of the sea. And every day, before he took the path up the mountain, he always notched up the date on the cottonwood tree by the clearing.

Eventually, his patience was rewarded. Late on the afternoon of 31 January 1709, two ships' masts pricked the edge of the horizon. Alexander waited. Slowly the ships came into view. He screwed up his eyes. Yes – these were definitely English ships! He threw his goatskin cap in the air and ran down the mountainside whooping with joy.

He didn't know it then, but the ships out in the bay were *The Duke* and *The Dutchess* on a mission to the Pacific under the command of Captain Woodes Rogers. The following day, Rogers signed up one goatskin-clad Scots savage as his new first mate. Alexander Selkirk had not merely been saved from loneliness and oblivion, he had been rescued by the captain of what was to be one of the most famous and successful privateering voyages of the 18th century. This time, at least, his nose had served him well.

MAP SHOWING THE COURSE OF
WOODES ROGERS'S
WORLD VOYAGE

ATLANTIC OCEAN

PACIFIC
OCEAN

LOWER
CALIFORNIA
Acapulco

From
Great
Britain

Towards the
Philippines

Galapagos
Islands

Guayaquil

BRAZIL

Juan
Fernandez
Island

CHILE

Rio de Janeiro

Cape Horn

CHAPTER SIX

For two weeks Captain Woodes Rogers and his men camped on Juan Fernandez and rested after their long, hard trip round the Horn. They tied sails to the tree trunks near the shore to form canopies and lay their scurvied men on beds of leaves underneath. With the fresh food and air, the sick recovered quickly. Only one sailor died – and he had already been toothless and limp as a rag-doll when they carried him ashore.

The beach, meanwhile, turned into a small, busy town, with men sawing wood and stretching out sails and hammering bits of metal on a makeshift forge. All day long the air was thick with the smell of curing meat and burning blubber. The sailors melted down 80 gallons of elephant seal fat to make oil for their lamps.

Alexander played the host. The sailors nicknamed him 'the governor' and he shared his knowledge willingly. He led the men to the turnip patches and the cabbage palms. He showed them the stream where the watercress grew and pointed out the best rock pools for finding crayfish. He made turnip top stew flavoured with parsley and pepper and kept the camp in fresh meat by catching two or three goats every day. The sailors marvelled at Alexander's speed – he could even outrun the ship's bulldog.

Finally, on 14th February (St Valentine's Day) 1709, *The Duke* and *The Dutchess* set sail, bound for the town of Guayaquil up the Peruvian coast and Alexander said goodbye to his island forever.

Alexander took some time to adjust to life aboard. He found his new shoes hurt his feet, and at mealtimes he would stare at the stale brown slurry in his bowl and remember with longing the watercress and succulent seal meat of Juan Fernandez. The first time he drank ale, he spat it out in disgust. And from then on the other seamen would laugh at the sour face he made as he downed his drink.

But slowly he adapted. His speech improved and he became less reserved – though he still kept to himself and he told no one how much he missed his cats. Every day, to retrain his eye, he fired his musket at the seagulls hovering overhead.

For days the sun shone and the ships sailed smoothly northwards. The journey seemed so easy that Captain Rogers remarked that it was as if the good Lord were parting the waters before them. The sailors passed these long, gentle hours lounging on the decks, fishing over the side and gambling. They bet on anything – from the turns of the wind to the next man to fall sick. Of course the seamen had little to wager – their booty was still just vain imagining. For now they would have to be content with making and losing invisible fortunes. The reckoning would come later.

***

Captain Woodes Rogers hated to see his men so lax and dissolute. One day he called a council of officers and banned all gambling. He ordered his midshipman to carve two wooden sticks to beat any sailor that took the Lord's name in vain. Every morning all hands were called to the quarterdeck for a church service.

The men grumbled that Rogers had become more chaplain than captain.

But the sailors' discontent soon vanished. For, as *The Duke* and *The Dutchess* made their way up the coast of South America, they met the Spanish ships. Woodes and his men started by taking two small coastal vessels, which put up no resistance. Then the privateers captured two larger ships, only one of which tried to fight back, (two privateers were killed in the skirmish – one was Captain Rogers's beloved younger brother, John). Finally another coaster fell to the privateers.

Each time the procedure was the same: the privateers would catch up with the enemy, board the ship and then relieve the passengers of their valuables before ushering them down into the hold. It was easy work. Gradually the ships and prisoners and slaves all accumulated, so that by the time the expedition neared Guayaquil, the privateers possessed a small fleet, and Alexander commanded his own little coaster.

Guayaquil was inland, some thirty miles up the river Guaya. So, having anchored their ships in the bay, the privateers sent on a squadron of small rowing boats to investigate. For two days they travelled upstream on the currents, spending the ebb tides bobbing in the hot, sticky shade of the Mangrove trees. Then, late on the second night, they came round the last corner of the river to find Guayaquil all alight. In the jumble of streets by the waterfront, lanterns and torches glowed. Up on the hill above the town a bonfire lit the night sky. Everywhere bells rang, muskets and cannons roared.

The town, it seemed, had been warned. Rogers was for immediate attack, but other officers, who argued that they would fare better by negotiating a ransom, outvoted the captain. So Rogers sent a boat to the shore with emissaries to agree a price for the town.

The bargaining was slow – for a day and a night small boats carried envoys to and fro from the riverbank. Alexander, sitting in his open boat with his feet swollen from the heat, looked on in disgust. He was a junior officer with no sway in the council – but surely his superiors weren't fools? If they waited any longer there would be nothing left in the town, not even a scrap of plate, or a twist of tobacco.

Just as Alexander was beginning to resign himself to another long day of waiting, he heard a shout from

Rogers's boat. The boats drew up alongside each other.

Captain Rogers's face was pale with exhaustion. He spoke abruptly: 'I have had enough of their delays and sweet-talking. Men make ready for the landing. We will attack directly. God's blessings be with you all.'

Alexander looked up to see the seamen pulling down the white flag and raising the English colours. On the shore a straggly line of militia took up half kneeling positions on the quayside. As the boats approached the shore, the Spanish soldiers' first shots rang out and the privateers crouched low in their boats and fired back.

When Alexander felt the keel scrape the slipway, he jumped out of the boat and ran up the shore, releasing all the pent-up rage from those long days sitting in the boat. Ahead of him the militia were already turning on their heels and making for the town. He raced after them, firing at their backs.

A minute later Alexander found himself leading a group of men up a narrow street facing a church. Ahead of him were a line of four small cannon – he was running *into* a line of fire, and the Spanish gunners, stepping back and covering their ears, were waiting for the explosion.

Suddenly the boom of the cannons filled the air. But Alexander kept on running, and none of the men around him stopped. The gunners looked up through the smoke, and, seeing that the cannons hadn't stopped their attackers, turned and fled. When the privateers reached the main square, it was empty.

John Connely, a young Irishman with dark blue eyes and a shock of curly hair, turned to Alexander and laughed. 'All gone! I swear there's not a man among them! They are soft as sows.'

But Alexander shook his head. 'Maybe,' he replied, 'but they're sly. We'll find little enough here for all our pains.'

The privateers prised open the great iron studded front doors of the church and walked into the cool, dark interior. Everything seemed tranquil and ordinary. But there were no priests. The altar gold was gone. There were no candlesticks, no silver baptism cup by the font. In the priests' apartments at the back, even the embroidered vestments had been spirited away.

All over the town, it was the same story. The privateers pulled at floorboards and forced open chests – but they found almost nothing of value. In the warehouses down by the water lay rolls of calico and sacks of cocoa and flour. There were vats of oil and cones of sugar, and the sailors could drink fine wine and brandy to their heart's content. But the gold was gone. The citizens of Guayaquil had filled their bags and cleared out.

Not everyone had left – the elderly and the poor had stayed behind, and soon the interpreter discovered that in fact, the town had not been forewarned of the privateers' arrival – the bonfires and lanterns had merely been in celebration of a local fete. But when the interpreter asked where the town's riches were, the Guayaquilenos just shrugged their shoulders and pointed to the wooded hills above the town. The riches were all upstream.

That first night, Alexander and Connely wandered back up from the warehouses rolling a keg of brandy between them, and stopping to drink the health of King William and Captain Rogers at every turn in the street. Eventually they staggered into the plaza. Here Alexander wiped the drink off his chin and looked up at a finely proportioned town house, with plaster curlicues and delicate wrought iron balconies.

'That's a grand house we have up there,' said Connely inspecting the crest over the door.

Alexander grinned, 'Shall we?'

The bolts on the front door gave way easily and the two men were soon in a dark tiled hallway with a wide elegant staircase. They ran upstairs and searched the rooms. But the parlour contained nothing of value except gilt furniture that was too heavy to take away. And in one of the bedchambers, they found a rosewood jewellery box, but it was empty.

Then, when they searched for the way down to the cellar, Connely opened a cupboard door under the stairs, pulled out an old bemused man, and held him up by his lapels so that his feet dangled uselessly in the air.

'The gold! Where is the gold hidden!' hissed Connely.

The old man stared back, his body quivering like a small bird.

Alexander came up and pressed his face up against the old man's nose 'Gold! Doro!' he shouted.

Possibly because of the brandy fumes, tears ran

down the old man's cheeks. He blinked hard and muttered something in Spanish that the privateers could not understand. Alexander shook him again. This time the old man pointed in the direction of the church and cried, 'Iglesia! Iglesia! Iglesia!'

Alexander and Connely made their way across the square, rolling their brandy keg before them. They pushed on the great church door, which swung open softly. As they entered the gloom of the church, Alexander felt a strange sense of foreboding.

He also smelt something horrible. Alexander had been in the church earlier and then there had been just the familiar musty overtones of old flowers and frankincense. But now he detected a sweet sickly stench, reminiscent of overhung meat, or rotting bandages.

Over in the far corner of the church some torches were burning and there rose a murmur of voices and the creak of splintering wood.

'I swear it stinks like a charnel house,' muttered Connely. The two men crept down the side of the church with their muskets cocked. As they came closer to the light, they saw that it was a group of their own seamen who were clearly busy sawing and prising bits of wood and pulling at long white sheets.

Alexander and Connely put away their muskets and stepped forward into the light of the torches. This was a fearful moment—and the terrible sight that met Alexander's eyes would haunt him till the day he died.

For now it was clear what was happening. The wood the seamen had been prising open belonged to coffins, and the sheets being tugged and pulled at were shrouds. Desperate for gold, these men had opened the floorboards and rummaged the graves of Guayaquilino. Strewn at their feet, was a jumble of yellowed, mouldering corpses.

The seamen stood up and grinned sheepishly – all except one man, MacKinnon, who was sitting on an upturned coffin intent on sawing the finger off a dead man with a gold signet ring. Alexander clutched the wretch by his hair, pulled him to his feet and struck him hard several times across the face.

The other seamen watched sulkily. They were the very dregs of *The Dutchess* – light-fingered Sickart, that quivering little toady Jones, and MacKinnon who had grassed up his own father and watched him swing from the gallows. Alexander looked at the motley group and felt a cold hand gripping on his heart.

'Put the bodies back,' he said quietly. Then he turned to Connely and added, 'We shall surely be cursed for this.'

Alexander slept badly that night – he wanted to leave the town as soon as possible. So when dawn broke and Captain Rogers asked for volunteers to sail further upstream in search of booty, he and Connely quickly offered their services. Later that morning they set off, taking with them an interpreter and a dozen men – hardworking fellows with honest faces and sturdy shoulders. The very thought of sharing a boat with the coffin-breakers made him shiver.

***

The river narrowed after Guayaquil and the men rowed on through the hazy heat of the afternoon, stopping to search the houses dotted along the riverbank, but finding little. The privateers' arms ached from all the rowing. Where, they wondered, could these people have hidden their gold?

It was Connely who heard the women's voices first. The privateers were pulling tight round a bend in the river when suddenly Connely put his fingers to his lips. Before them lay a small wooden jetty leading to two villas set back from the river. On the veranda of one of the villas, were two dark-haired young women dressed in bright silks, and engaged in animated conversation.

Quietly the men moored the boat and crept up the path towards the house. After sending some men round to block off any back exits, Connely and Alexander then knocked on the door. The maid, a simpering little thing in a cambric bonnet, opened the front door, let out a squeal of fright and scuttled away. A minute later she re-emerged with the two women they had just seen on the veranda – but now their faces were pale and stony.

Alexander turned to the interpreter and told him to give their compliments to the ladies and explain that they meant them no harm. When the interpreter had finished, the women nodded stiffly to the privateers and beckoned them upstairs. Alexander, who had never before been admitted into a gentle-woman's house by the front door, entered a small ornate parlour and saw before him more riches than any privateer could dream of. For there were not two, but 12 young ladies in the parlour. Twelve young ladies all with gold earrings and with the finest bracelets and gold necklaces and tiny jewel-encrusted bags.

Alexander told the interpreter to ask the ladies to be so kind as to remove their jewellery. Buckles were unclasped, clips undone, and gradually Alexander's upturned hat became heavy with gold. If one of the women lingered over the task, he would flash a dangerous, glittering smile and each time the woman would hastily cast off her remaining jewellery.

Alexander found it hard to take his eyes off these women. They wore such fine clothes, draped so loosely over their bodies. He could see the outline of their hips and bosoms under the thin drapes. Yet he was also puzzled – for there was something a little strange about the shape of these women. The small woman in crimson, whom he had seen on the veranda, was bending over a mirror while she removed a pin from her hair. Her dress did not fall smoothly on her back. She looked lumpy as a sack of coal.

Alexander beckoned the woman over and, blushing heavily, she came and stood in front of him. Everyone watched in silence as Alexander ran his hand down the side of the woman's body. When he reached her waist there was a faint jingling noise.

Alexander stopped, his head rocked back and he let out a roar of laughter. The woman smiled sheepishly, and fiddled with her clothing until a bundle of gold and silver chains and strings of pearls dropped heavily to the ground beneath her.

'Why Madam,' Alexander exclaimed, 'You are a champion pack horse!'

Two more gold chains clattered to the ground.

'I declare we must pat all the ladies now!' Connely shouted.

And thus, with a nervous titter from the ladies, the great jewellery rummage began. Alexander and Connely stroked and patted and coaxed each of the young ladies in turn. They were most surprised by some of their discoveries. Connely snorted with laughter when he found one woman had two solid-gold serving platters tied to her midriff, and the petticoat of another young woman turned out to contain a multitude of small purses.

As the privateers collected up the jewellery, they seemed to relieve the women of their fears. The young ladies began to smile and flutter their fans. The less gold they carried the more they giggled.

It was a slow and delicate business. The afternoon

wore on and eventually the little simpering maid came curtseying with a tray of small glasses of claret.

The interpreter reported that the ladies, as a gesture of thanks to the privateers for their 'gentlemanly conduct', wished the men to stay and dine.

Later that evening, when the claret was all drunk and candles were guttering, the privateers finally bade farewell to the ladies and, carrying two wooden boxes of jewellery (for Alexander's hat had long ceased to suffice) they made their way back to the boat. As they set off back down the river, Alexander looked back a little wistfully at the house, with its upstairs windows still glowing with candlelight. He spied a figure on the veranda and looked again more closely. It was the dark-eyed young lady in crimson.

CHAPTER SEVEN

The privateers left Guayaquil, with their guns and drums pounding into the hot morning mist. They took with them the warehouse goods and the ladies' fine jewellery and hostages for ransom. But they also took an invisible, and deadly, extra gift.

For, just days after they had turned the ship back out West into the Pacific, a terrible epidemic struck the privateers. Many believed it was a Divine punishment for desecrating the crypt in the church. Certainly, by digging up the corpses, the privateers brought the disease upon themselves, for Guayaquil had recently suffered an outbreak of plague.

Alexander, who had been put in command of one of the small coasters that served as the hospital ship, was inundated with patients. Down in the half-light of the hold the air reeked of vinegar and brimstone, and everywhere sick men lay in rows in their hammocks. The physicians applied cold presses and leeches, but there was little anyone could do. No amount of hot punch or Venice treacle could pull a man through the worst of the fever.

Eighteen men died. Alexander and his crew prepared the bodies in the traditional way. They placed a coin on each eye and bound the jaw shut with a strip of cloth. Then, having put a cannon ball at the dead man's head and foot, they wrapped each corpse in a sail and sewed the shroud up. Just to make sure that the poor wretch was truly dead, they always passed the last stitch through the corpse's nose. Then they cast the body overboard.

After 500 miles of sailing, the privateers finally arrived at the great black rock islands of the Galapagos in the Pacific Ocean. Here they made tents on the shore for the sick, and collected turtles and huge quantities of fish. But the land was barren, they found no water and one of the smaller boats with five privateers went missing.

Dispirited, the privateers sailed back east towards the rain-drenched islands of Gorgona, near the South

American mainland, where they restocked with water and refitted the ships. They then returned once more to the Galapagos islands, to search for their lost friends – but could find no trace of them.

In September, they headed north across the Gulf of Panama and past Acapulco in Mexico. And at last, on 1st November, they reached their goal – the coast of California. Here the privateers would try for the biggest and richest prize of all – the treasured Manila galleon that each year carried all the trade from the Far East for the King of Spain.

The galleon's route and timing was well known – the ship, or ships (for sometimes the goods were divided between two vessels) left Manila in the Philippines in the spring, made the long, hard crossing of the Northern Pacific and then, at the end of the year, came down the West coast of America and into the harbour at Acapulco. All the privateers had to do was lie in wait.

For seven weeks, the ships patrolled the coast. At first the privateers guzzled like aldermen on the turtles that they had filled their ships with back on the Galapagos, but soon supplies ran out and the men were reduced to eating broiled fish, and the occasional dolphin. Sometimes the long-haired savages on the coast brought them some game. The hare was very popular. But nobody, not even the starving young cabin lads, fancied roast fox.

More importantly bread and biscuit were running low. Rogers ordered the pursers to re-count the biscuit barrels, and on 20th December the captain wrote the tally in his ledger. The ships held 70 days' worth of provisions. They needed at least 50 days to cross the Pacific. He called in the officers, and together they glumly resolved to abandon their waiting, and simply refit the ships and head for home.

Alexander slept poorly that night, even though he had drunk heavily – for the men had broken open a hogshead of ale to wash down their disappointment. In the morning he lay in his hammock, his sore head aching more with every roll of the ship. Then, suddenly, there came a shout that dispelled all his malaise. It was not the call to watch, but a cry from the man at the mast-head. A sail! Seven leagues out to sea!

Alexander staggered out on to the quarterdeck. Half a dozen seamen were already climbing the ratlines to see for themselves. Captain Rogers, running out of his cabin, adjusted his wig and shouted to the mate to clear the anchor and raise the French ensign. Rogers saw Alexander looking at him and winked.

'Mr Selkirk, we do ourselves a disservice should we scare her away with the English colours.'

'Aye sir,' replied Alexander with a nod.

The Duke pulled up anchor and set sail. All day she followed the galleon – but there was little wind and the ship moved sluggishly. In the afternoon, Rogers ordered the gunner to fire a salute. The ship from Manila, still a tiny silhouette on the horizon, fired back.

By evening *The Duke* had still not caught up, and *The Dutchess* was still further behind. But they could see the Spanish ship well now. Alexander was surprised. After all he had heard about the Manila galleons, he had expected a great towering, 1,000-ton "man of war", but this one was just a sturdy frigate.

All night the privateers laboured. Men took turns to work the ship's paddles, and every hour *The Duke* inched a little closer to her quarry. Down in the gun deck the noise was deafening – bulwarks being smashed down by the carpenter to clear the decks, cannons creaking as they were rolled into place, and gun ports being heaved open. Over the din the officers barked commands and the men cursed and ran in every direction.

Alexander's voice soon grew hoarse. He didn't, he realised later, feel frightened. He didn't consider that he might soon die. All he knew was that if they forgot just one small thing – if they didn't get enough buckets of water ready, if the wet sand and sawdust weren't strewn on every corner of the decks, if the powder boys didn't get the cannon balls cleaned, if the gunner didn't make up enough cartridges – if just one of these details were overlooked, than all could be lost.

At eight o'clock in the morning the preparations were finally complete and the men could stop to rest. The Manila ship was now well within range of the guns and she too was ready for battle, with her guns out and huge powder barrels hanging from her yard-arms to stop the privateers from boarding.

On the gun deck of *The Duke*, cook served up a kettle of hot chocolate. The men cupped their hands round their tankards and slurped the thick sweet liquid, glad for the warmth in their bellies. There was a sharp banging and the men looked up. Captain

Rogers, standing on an upturned bucket, raised his hand to call for silence. In a solemn tone he read Psalm 121, 'I will lift up mine eyes unto the hills.'

Then he called for the men to join him in the Lord's Prayer and a dull rumble of voices started up in the half-light of the gun deck.

But the prayer was never finished. The men had just asked to be 'forgiven their trespasses', when the Spanish guns roared out and a thunderous crash shook the ship, sending splinters of wood flying across the bows. Captain Rogers snapped his prayer book closed and the men scattered in all directions, some to the cannons in the gun deck, others up on to the quarterdeck.

Alexander ran to the forehatch. The Spanish ship was ahead of them, with smoke still swirling round her gun ports. A breeze had finally begun to stir. So he shouted out orders to trim the sails and sent two men up the ratlines to fix the topsails. To get The Duke up broadsides with the Spanish ship, he must catch the wind immediately. If their quarry slipped away now, he would never be able to hold his head up in any Bristol tavern.

While a hail of bullets hit the deck, Alexander

shouted at the hands to pull harder on the ropes. Down below he could hear the officer in charge of the gunners bellowing out his commands.

'Aim!' he shouted. Then: 'Fire!'

After a barely perceptible pause, there came a thunderous roar that shook every board of the ship. The Spanish cannons responded a minute later. Cannon boomed overhead, striking at the rigging, ripping through ratlines and sail. One ball crashed at the foot of the foremast and smouldered into a small fire until the boatswain ran over with a bucket of wet sand to put out the flames. A minute later *The Duke*'s cannons fired again. The gunners' aim was truer this time – the cannons ripped through the Spanish decks, making great black holes by the gunports.

Alexander gestured to the seamen at the wheel to move in nearer to the wind. *The Duke* was coming up alongside the Spanish ship. Now the men could aim more sharply with their muskets – for the two ships were barely a few yards apart.

Alexander could make out the faces of the Spanish sailors. Now that *The Duke* was in place he had time to use his own gun. He leant against the rack of hammocks piled up by the rails, aimed at a man halfway up the enemy rigging and fired. The man fell, his scream downed by the blare of guns. Alexander felt satisfied and quickly reloaded. All those hours of potting seagulls was finally paying off.

The battle intensified, Alexander could barely breathe for the smoke. All around him came the cracking of muskets and the cries of the men, and then every few minutes a great, deafening boom from the cannons shook both the ships. And yet, for all the din and confusion, things were becoming clearer to him. The Spanish certainly had a better ship – often the cannon just bounced off her hull like peashot – and her gunners were good, steady workers. But they were hired hands, and not desperadoes like Rogers's men. The privateers were firing far faster. For every three cracks of the Spanish cannon, *The Duke* gave five. As a result, they were hitting the Spanish harder. So far there was only one man wounded on *The Duke*, whereas he had seen a couple of bad fires in the Spanish gun deck and several falls from the enemy rigging – one of which he could boast was his own doing.

More importantly, *The Dutchess*, which had lagged behind for so long, was finally catching up. She came up on the far side of the Spanish galleon. And now, for the first time, her big guns rang out across the water.

Then Alexander heard a commotion behind him. He turned to see Captain Rogers propped up against a chest, with blood streaming from his mouth. His left cheek was a gory, mashed pulp, with shards of jawbone sticking through the wound. The poor man's teeth lay in a pool of blood on the deck. He tried to speak, but all that came out was a horrible choked gurgle.

Alexander put his hand on the captain's arm – a liberty he would never have dared to take under normal circumstances.

'What would you have us do? Sir.' he asked.

But Rogers paid no heed, and although blood was still streaming down his front, his eyes were shining, and his mouth – or what was left of his mouth – was smiling. He made another gurgling noise, lifted an arm and pointed.

Alexander turned to follow his gaze. Now he understood the Captain's delight. For, on the Spanish ship, the great red and white and gold battle flag of the *Real Armada* was slowly being lowered. The Manila galleon had surrendered.

'She's ours! She's ours!' shouted Alexander, with

tears of relief smarting in his eyes. The men put down their arms and hugged each other. If they survived the long, hard journey home, they would be rich men. But now there was work to do. They must collect their prisoners, they must rummage, and they must refit.

While the seamen lowered a rowing boat into the water, Captain Rogers slowly gathered up his teeth.

CHAPTER EIGHT

Over the years Reverend Tulloch of Largo had refined his talent for terrifying the simple people of his parish. He had even made a pact with himself that he would never end a sermon until he had seen at least one member of his congregation shake with fear. Shivering with cold – for his little church was dank and draughty – didn't count. Nor did tears. He needed the satisfaction of seeing someone truly scared out of their wits.

Today, on a cold winter's Sunday, nobody had yet succumbed. So Reverend Tulloch ranted on, reminding the bowed heads in front of him of the terrible sufferings of hell, the eternal fires, the plagues of scorpions, the boils and brimstone.

Suddenly, there was movement at the back of the

church. The door opened and a stranger, dressed in lace and gold cloth, entered. The stranger settled himself down in one of the back pews, turned a broad, weather-beaten face to the pulpit and smiled at the minister.

For just a moment Reverend Tulloch faltered. Then his voice thundered on – though his miserable congregation were now all shuffling and craning their necks.

Mrs Selcraig, sitting by her husband John, stared at the newcomer. Like everyone in the church she sized up his clothes: the gold embroidery, the slightly skewed periwig, the lacy cuffs, none too white but clearly expensive.

The stranger seemed a gentleman, yet his face was brown as a nutmeg and his coat oddly short, like a seaman's. She screwed up her eyes to look closer, there was something familiar about the face – that broad smile, the wide cheek bones, those bright blue eyes.

Mrs Selcraig put her hand to her mouth and let out a little scream. She stumbled out of her seat, barged past her husband, and ran down the aisle. She clasped the stranger's head between her hands and kissed him.

'My boy! My blessed boy!' she cried, as she hugged her long lost son.

Then the whole village was on its feet, crowding round. Alexander Selkirk had been away ten years, and had long been given up for dead. Now everyone wanted to look at him, to hear him speak, to finger his rich clothes. He was almost lifted off his feet by the press of people, as everyone spilled outside into the cold morning sunlight.

Reverend Tulloch, still standing at his pulpit, watched open-mouthed as the last of his parishioners filed out the door. For once in his life he was lost for words.

POSTSCRIPT

Alexander Selkirk never settled back into life in Largo. Eventually he went south again, got married and returned to sea. In 1721 he died from tropical fever on a navy ship off the coast of Gambia. He was then 45 years old – a ripe old age for an 18th-century seaman – and quite a rich man. His will mentions four gold rings, one silver tobacco box, a gold-headed walking stick, a pair of gold candlesticks, a silver-hilted sword, and various naval books and instruments. For more than a hundred years his descendants still kept his sea-chest, and a coconut shell cup, and his brown stoneware tankard.

Today all his possessions have sadly vanished. In the village of Largo the only memento is a small statue of Selkirk in his goatskins.

On Juan Fernandez he is better remembered. 'Robinson Crusoe Island', as it is now called, today belongs to Chile. In Selkirk's bay lies the village of San Juan Bautista, where the inhabitants make their living from fishing the huge local lobsters. Above the village loom the mountains. The path up is steep and stony, but eventually it opens out into a small clearing marked with a shrine and a plaque.

Here was Alexander Selkirk's lookout point, where every day he would come to wait and watch and hope.

History is written for and by the rich and powerful. We know about the kings and queens of the past, but the lives of ordinary people are much more of a mystery. Alexander Selkirk, the son of a humble shoemaker, is an exception. We have reports about him throughout his life: church records, court hearings and the memoirs of the men who found him on Juan Fernandez. And the reason why Selkirk's life was so well documented is simple: he was constantly getting into trouble and causing a stir.

1676 – Selkirk is born in the village of Largo, in Fife, Scotland.

1689 – Selkirk, aged 13, is reported to the authorities for throwing stones in the church ground.

1695 – Selkirk is again in trouble for 'indecent conduct in church'. He runs off to sea.

1701 – Selkirk returns to Largo. He is now an experienced seaman.

1703 – Selkirk is yet again in trouble with the church after a family brawl. He returns to sea. In Bristol he joins the *Cinque Ports* as sailing master and sets off for South America.

1704 – Selkirk argues with the captain of his ship and is left behind on Juan Fernandez island.

1709 – Selkirk is rescued. He joins Woodes Rogers' privateering expedition and continues to sail round the world.

1710 – Selkirk returns to Britain.

1713 – Now living in Bristol, Selkirk is charged with assaulting a shipwright. There are no records of whether he is sentenced.

1718 – Selkirk joins a naval warship *HMS Weymouth* as first mate and travels around the south coast of England.

1720 – Selkirk marries a widow called Frances Candis.

1721 – Selkirk sails to the Gold Coast on *HMS Weymouth*. He dies of a fever off the coast of Gambia.

Author biography

Amanda Mitchison is a feature writer for the
Sunday Telegraph Magazine. She lives in Bristol
and has two young sons.

OTHER TITLES IN THE **WHO WAS...** SERIES

Emily Davison
The girl who gave her life for her cause
Claudia FitzHerbert
1-904095-66-6

Sam Johnson
The wonderful word doctor
Andrew Billen
1-904095-77-1

Ada Lovelace
The computer wizard of Victorian England
Lucy Lethbridge
1-904095-76-3

Annie Oakley
Sharpshooter of the Wild West
Lucy Lethbridge
1-904095-60-7

Charlotte Brontë
The girl who turned her life into a book
Kate Hubbard
1-904095-80-1

Ned Kelly
Gangster hero of the Australian outback
Charlie Boxer
1-904095-61-5

William Shakespeare
The mystery of the world's greatest playwright
Rupert Christiansen
1-904095-81-X

Queen Victoria
The woman who ruled the world
Kate Hubbard
1-904095-82-2

Florence Nightingale
The lady with the lamp
Charlotte Moore
1-904095-83-6

Madame Tussaud
Waxwork queen of the French Revolution
Tony Thorne
1-904095-85-2

Nelson Mandela
The prisoner who became a president
Adrian Hadland
1-904095-86-0

The Bloody Baron
Evil invader of the East
Nick Middleton
1-904095-87-9

WHO WAS... Admiral Nelson
The Sailor Who Dared All to Win
Sam Llewellyn
1-904095-65-8

No one ever imagined that a weak skinny boy like Horatio Nelson would be able to survive the hardships of life at sea. But he did. In fact he grew up to become a great naval hero, the man who saved Britain from invasion by the dreaded Napoleon.

Nelson was someone who always did things his own way. He lost an eye and an arm in battle, but never let that hold him back. He was brilliant on ships, clumsy on land, ferocious in battle, knew fear but overcame it, and never, never took no for an answer.

This is his story.

WHO WAS... David Livingstone
The Legendary Explorer
Amanda Mitchison
1-904095-84-4

Born a poor Glasgow cotton-mill worker, David grew
up to become a great explorer and hero of his time.

This is his incredible story. The tough man of Victorian
Britain would stop at nothing in his determination to
be the first white man to explore Afirca, even if it
meant dragging his wife and children along with him.

He trekked hundreds of miles through dangerous terri-
tory, braving terrible illness and pain, and was attacked
by cannibals, rampaging lions and killer ants...

WHO WAS... Anne Boleyn
The Queen Who Lost her Head
Laura Beatty
1-904095-78-X

For Anne Boleyn, King Henry VIII threw away his
wife, outraged his people, chucked his religion,
and drove his best friend to death.

What does it take to drive a King this crazy?
Was she a witch? An enchantress? Whatever she was,
Anne turned Tudor England upside-down and shook it.
And everyone was talking about her...

But Anne lived dangerously. And when she could
not give the King the one thing he wanted – a son –
his love went out like a light. The consequences
for Anne were deadly...